Learn by Handwriting

Practice Workbook

Numbers from 1 to 50

Numbers and Words

memorescribe.com

Our Advantage

Numbers from 1 to 50 - Numbers and Words - Print 2
Memorescribe Learn by Handwriting Practice Workbook
Copyright © 2024 by Globaloft, LLC
Alpharetta, GA

Publishing Credits | Authors, Editors, Interior & Cover Designers: Jessica Cobo and Victor Cobo

Memorescribe Product # N150P2PE

No part of this publication may be reproduced, stored in a retrieval system, or transmitted in any form or by any means—electronic, mechanical, photocopying, recording, scanning, or otherwise—except as permitted under Sections 107 or 108 of the 1976 United States Copyright Act, without the prior written permission of Globaloft, LLC. Requests to Globaloft, LLC for permission should be addressed to info@globaloft.com.

Limit of Liability/Disclaimer of Warranty: While the publisher and author have used their best efforts in preparing this book, they make no representations or warranties with respect to the accuracy or completeness of the contents of this work and specifically disclaim all warranties, including without limitation warranties of fitness for a particular purpose. No warranty may be created or extended by sales or promotional materials. The advice and strategies contained herein may not be suitable for every situation. This work is sold with the understanding that the publisher is not engaged in rendering medical, legal, or other professional advice or services. If professional assistance is required, the services of a competent professional person should be sought. Neither the publisher nor the author shall be liable for damages arising herefrom, any loss of profit or any other commercial damages, including but not limited to special, incidental, consequential, or other damages. The fact that an individual, organization, or website is referred to in this work as a citation or potential source of further information does not mean that the author or publisher endorses the information the individual, organization, or website may provide or recommendations they/it may make. Further, readers should be aware that websites listed in this work may have changed or disappeared between when this work was written and when it was read.

For general information on our other products and services or to obtain technical support for Memorescribe workbooks, please visit our website at www.memorescribe.com.

Globaloft, LLC publishes its books in a variety of electronic and print formats. Some content that appears in print may not be available in electronic books and vice versa. For more information, please visit our website at www.memorescribe.com.

Trademarks: All trademarks are the property of their respective owners. Globaloft, LLC is not associated with any product or vendor mentioned in this book.

Memorescribe offers customized themes and content for commercial, educational, and religious organizations. Also, we offer discounts on bulk orders for charities, fundraising, education, missionaries, and churches. For more information please contact us at customedition@memorescribe.com.

TABLE OF CONTENTS

Dearest Persevering Writer,

One of my proudest achievements at the age of 8 was learning to read and write in cursive. Learning cursive whisked me away on adventures as I read my grandparents' beautiful handwritten travel postcards. Even today, I cherish my grandmother's handwritten recipe card as well as her personalized book inscriptions that I have the chance to re-read as I pass those books along to my children.

Many of us can remember the time before handwriting was eclipsed by digital communication. Consider the present reality, all the text messages and emails we read but barely remember and rarely keep as a treasured memory. While there are innumerable benefits to computer use and digital communication, handwriting remains a powerful, valuable skill.

Memorescribe Learn by Handwriting workbooks began as a passion project. When working to help my child develop handwriting skills, I discovered an opportunity to use handwriting practice time to learn and reinforce important educational information. Memorescribe workbooks offer you the opportunity to practice and develop your personal, unique handwriting style while taking advantage of the time to learn something new or reinforce information you learned in the past.

Wherever you are on your journey, no matter your age or handwriting ability, my hope is that Memorescribe's Learn by Handwriting workbooks will send you off on your own learning adventures, travelling as far as your handwriting will take you.

Jessica

Welcome to Memorescribe

Memorescribe Learn by Handwriting workbooks create a fun and meaningful opportunity to commit educational information to memory while you practice your handwriting because we believe handwriting is an invaluable skill. **Learn as you write with Memorescribe!**

IMPORTANCE OF HANDWRITING

1. Writing by hand is a **foundational educational skill** connected to academic progress and success.

2. Writing by hand **activates** different parts of **the brain** and can **boost** your **brain function.**

3. Writing by hand helps to **develop** the **small movements** and **coordination skills** needed **for success in everyday life.**

4. Handwriting notes helps to **organize thoughts** and **process information** more **deeply** which can lead to **better learning,** understanding, **retaining,** and recalling **information.**

5. A unique form of personal expression, handwriting can **display individual personality,** creative tendencies, and artistic craftsmanship as well as **verify identity.**

6. Writing by hand can help to **process emotions, set goals,** soothe and calm while encouraging **personal reflection** on experiences and circumstances.

7. Handwritten notes and documents convey a **memorable,** meaningful, **personal touch** and **demonstrate care** and thoughtfulness towards the recipient.

8. Preserving methods and styles of handwriting allows people groups and cultures the opportunity to **maintain heritage** and **safeguard history.**

Print and Cursive Handwriting

Print Handwriting, also known as Manuscript, is patterned after the style of letters commonly used in printed materials such as books, newspapers, or magazines. Each letter is written independently and is not connected to any other letter. To create print style handwriting, the writer lifts the pen or pencil from the paper after forming each letter. Print handwriting is simple and can often be easier to read than cursive style writing.

Cursive Handwriting is also known as Script, longhand, or joined-up writing. The scripted style of writing is created using connected, flowing letters which allows for faster, more elegant writing than print. Writers of cursive use single strokes to create letters without lifting the pen or pencil from the paper and connect the letters within the same word. Cursive handwriting is more intricate than print and can add a touch of sophistication whenever used.

With **Memorescribe, you can choose your handwriting style and text size.** For handwriting style, choose between print and cursive. For handwriting text size, choose from level 1, level 2, or level 3 in your selected style.

Workbooks are available in the following style and size options:

Books available in English, Spanish, and other languages.

Pencil Grip Tip:

Pinch the pencil between your thumb and first finger. Rest the pinched fingers with pencil on the middle finger. Curl the last two fingers into the palm of your hand for support as you rest your hand on the writing surface.

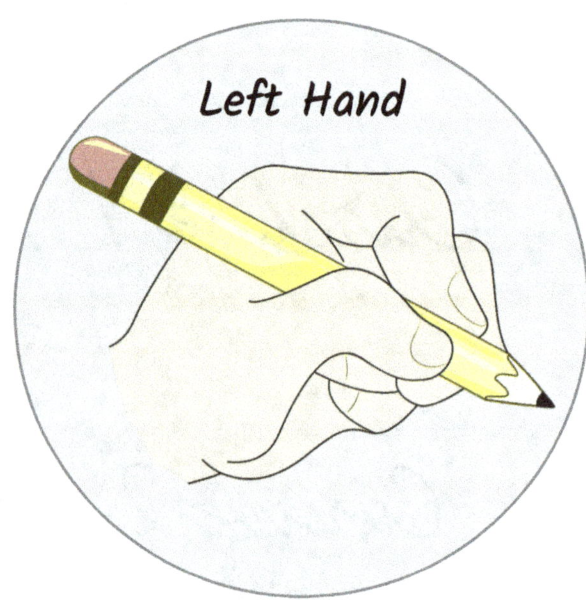

Supportive Handwriting Pencil Grip

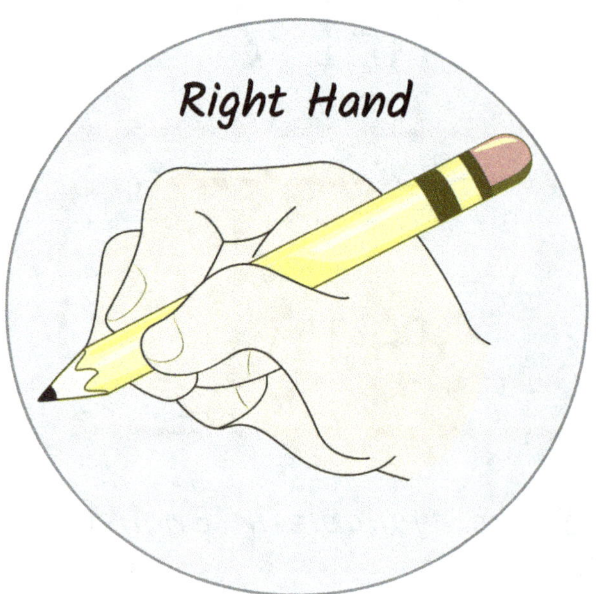

PRACTICE MAKES THE MASTER

Numbers from 1 to 50

1 One	11 Eleven	21 Twenty-one	31 Thirty-one	41 Forty-one
2 Two	12 Twelve	22 Twenty-two	32 Thirty-two	42 Forty-two
3 Three	13 Thirteen	23 Twenty-three	33 Thirty-three	43 Forty-three
4 Four	14 Fourteen	24 Twenty-four	34 Thirty-four	44 Forty-four
5 Five	15 Fifteen	25 Twenty-five	35 Thirty-five	45 Forty-five
6 Six	16 Sixteen	26 Twenty-six	36 Thirty-six	46 Forty-six
7 Seven	17 Seventeen	27 Twenty-seven	37 Thirty-seven	47 Forty-seven
8 Eight	18 Eighteen	28 Twenty-eight	38 Thirty-eight	48 Forty-eight
9 Nine	19 Nineteen	29 Twenty-nine	39 Thirty-nine	49 Forty-nine
10 Ten	20 Twenty	30 Thirty	40 Forty	50 Fifty

Numbers and Words

1 One - 2 Two - 3 Three

1 One - 2 Two - 3 Three

4 Four - 5 Five - 6 Six

4 Four - 5 Five - 6 Six

1

2

3

4

5

6

7

8

9

10

11

12

13

7 Seven - 8 Eight - 9 Nine

7 Seven - 8 Eight - 9 Nine

Numbers 1 to 50

memorescribe.com

10 Ten   -   11 Eleven   -   12 Twelve

10 Ten   -   11 Eleven   -   12 Twelve

Numbers 1 to 50

memorescribe.com

13 Thirteen   -   14 Fourteen

1

2

3

4

5

6

7

8

9

10

11

12

13

13 Thirteen   -   14 Fourteen

15 Fifteen - 16 Sixteen

15 Fifteen - 16 Sixteen

17 Seventeen - 18 Eighteen

17 Seventeen   -   18 Eighteen

19 Nineteen   -   20 Twenty

19 Nineteen   -   20 Twenty

1

2

3

4

5

6

7

8

9

10

11

12

13

21 Twenty-one - 22 Twenty-two

21 Twenty-one   -   22 Twenty-two

23 Twenty-three   24 Twenty-four

23 Twenty-three   24 Twenty-four

Numbers 1 to 50

memorescribe.com

Directions:

Search to find the list of words hidden inside the puzzle. Words can go in any direction and can share letters.

```
Y P K B T O X M T D J A J V
S E V E N H Q H W U I P I S
G D T D E Q I Y E Y Y V O L
N W P H E R M R N V T S Y G
C G A X T P R T T M L F V M
Q L H Y E Q H B Y E P E I R
H D S V N G A I O W E W W F
T I V M I E R M N Y U N E T
X O S E N H T A E K E X P I
I Z J A R E V I F Y T R O F
V T H I R T Y N I N E B P S
R U O F Y T R O F Z Y M F S
S O J T W E N T Y T H R E E
W D O E P F N Y L D V N L E
```

EIGHT   FIFTY   FORTY-FIVE   FORTY-FOUR

NINETEEN   SEVEN   THIRTEEN   THIRTY-NINE

THIRTY-SIX   TWELVE   TWENTY-ONE   TWENTY-THREE

Directions: Use the clues below to discover the missing words. Words share letters where they cross in the puzzle.

ACROSS

4. The number of days in the month of December

5. The number of fingers on one hand

6. The number of eyes in a group of ten people

7. The number of eggs in three dozen

DOWN

1. The number of hours in two days

2. The number of months in a year

3. The number of wheels in a pair of roller skates

25 Twenty-five - 26 Twenty-six

1

2

3

4

5

6

7

8

9

10

11

12

13

25 Twenty-five - 26 Twenty-six

27 Twenty-seven - 28 Twenty-eight

27 Twenty-seven - 28 Twenty-eight

29 Twenty-nine   -   30 Thirty

29 Twenty-nine   -   30 Thirty

31 Thirty-one - 32 Thirty-two

31 Thirty-one   -   32 Thirty-two

33 Thirty-three - 34 Thirty-four

33 Thirty-three - 34 Thirty-four

35 Thirty-five   -   36 Thirty-six

35 Thirty-five   -   36 Thirty-six

37 Thirty-seven   -   38 Thirty-eight

1

2

3

4

5

6

7

8

9

10

11

12

13

37 Thirty-seven - 38 Thirty-eight

Numbers 1 to 50

memorescribe.com

39 Thirty-nine - 40 Forty

39 Thirty-nine   -   40 Forty

41 Forty-one   -   42 Forty-two

41 Forty-one   -   42 Forty-two

43 Forty-three - 44 Forty-four

43 Forty-three - 44 Forty-four

45 Forty-five   -   46 Forty-six

45 Forty-five   -   46 Forty-six

47 Forty-seven - 48 Forty-eight

47 Forty-seven   -   48 Forty-eight

49 Forty-nine   -   50 Fifty

49 Forty-nine   -   50 Fifty

Break Activity 3
Word Search

Directions:

Search to find the list of words hidden inside the puzzle.
Words can go in any direction and can share letters.

```
W  E  C  A  X  T  Q  Y  Y  I  B  Y  W  L
W  I  N  U  W  V  B  B  J  F  H  Q  N  T
K  G  H  E  S  I  X  T  E  E  N  F  L  P
N  H  N  R  V  Y  V  W  S  L  X  U  X  E
V  T  U  R  T  E  W  C  E  I  X  C  V  K
Y  E  Z  N  U  W  S  B  W  Y  G  I  U  S
J  E  K  E  S  O  E  Y  Z  H  F  P  D  J
N  N  K  B  L  C  F  N  T  Y  W  P  T  D
E  U  E  E  R  H  T  Y  T  R  I  H  T  T
T  X  L  R  V  M  A  R  T  Y  O  O  G  H
F  O  R  T  Y  N  I  N  E  N  T  F  N  R
D  J  W  L  E  H  H  E  H  D  E  W  H  E
I  A  Y  R  T  O  K  Z  E  Y  F  W  O  E
V  T  H  G  I  E  Y  T  R  I  H  T  T  V
```

Directions: Use the clues below to discover the missing words. Words share letters where they cross in the puzzle.

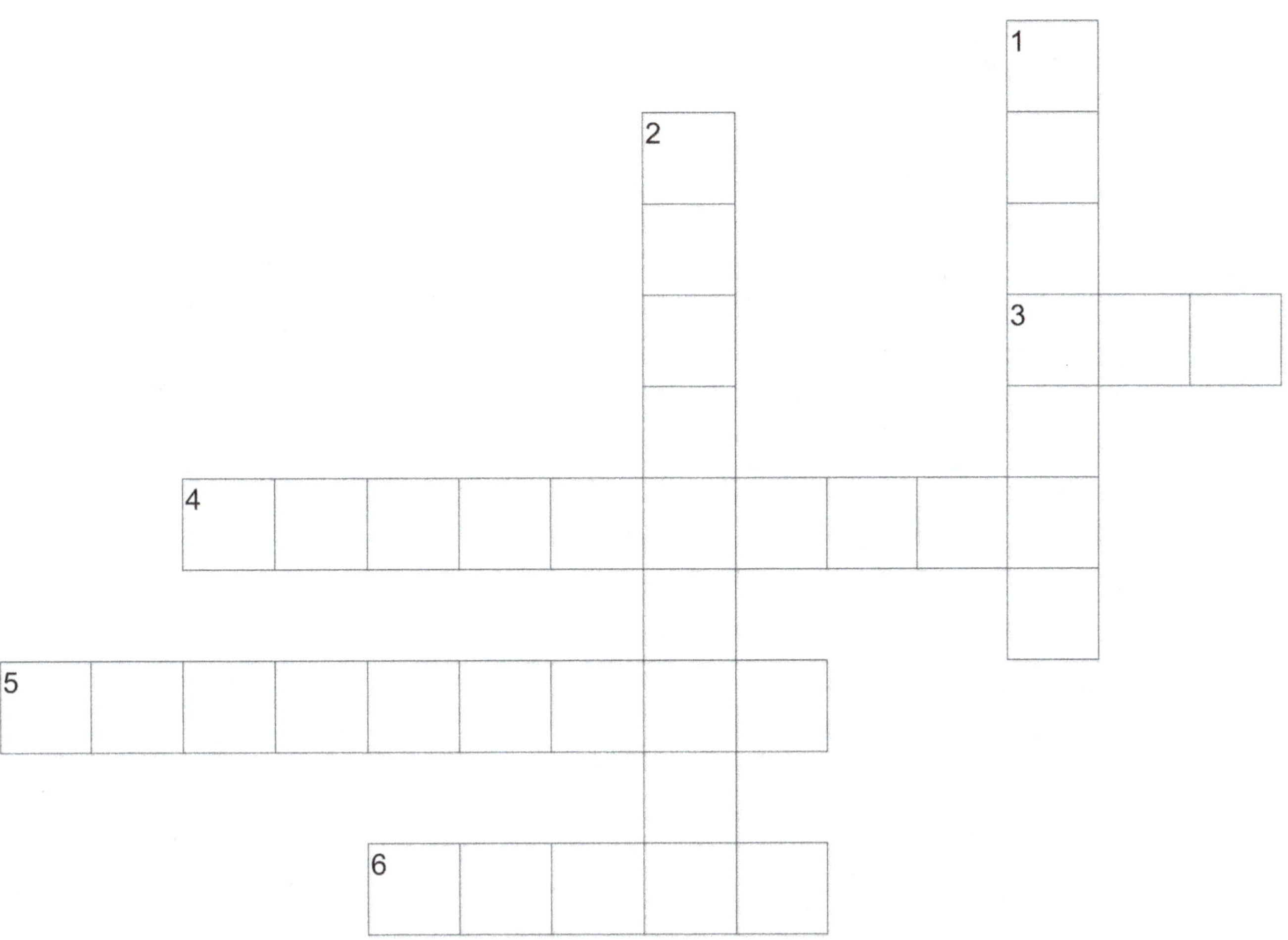

ACROSS

3. The number of toes on both feet combined

4. The number of days in five weeks

5. Half the number of weeks of the year

6. The number of letters in the name of the first month of the year

DOWN

1. The number half way between 0 and 30

2. The number half way between 40 and 50

Break Activities Solutions

Break Activity 1 - Page 30: **Word Search**

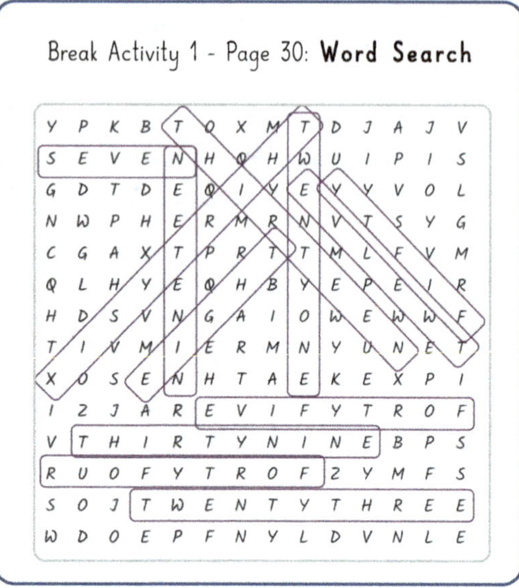

Break Activity 3 - Page 58: **Word Search**

Break Activity 2 - Page 31: **Crossword**

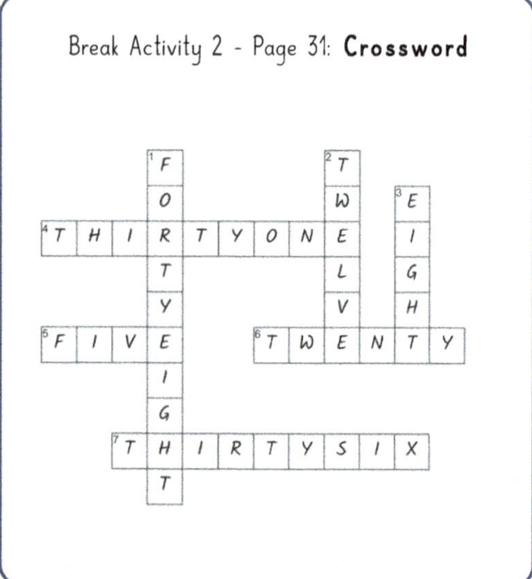

Break Activity 4 - Page 59: **Crossword**

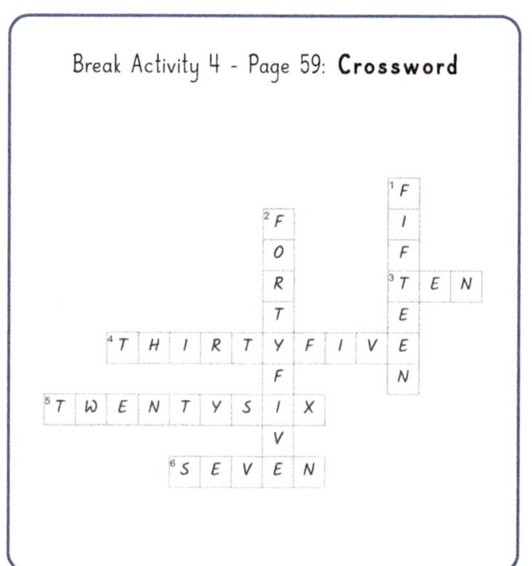

Memorescribe Workbook Themes

Family

Nature

Math

Manners

Faith

Science

World

Sports

General Knowledge

and more to come!

Contact us for customized content for your organization or project.

SINGLE
And
READY TO
mingle

DON'T GET
EVEN - GET
EVERYTHING

DIVORCED AF

Bye Bye
Marriage

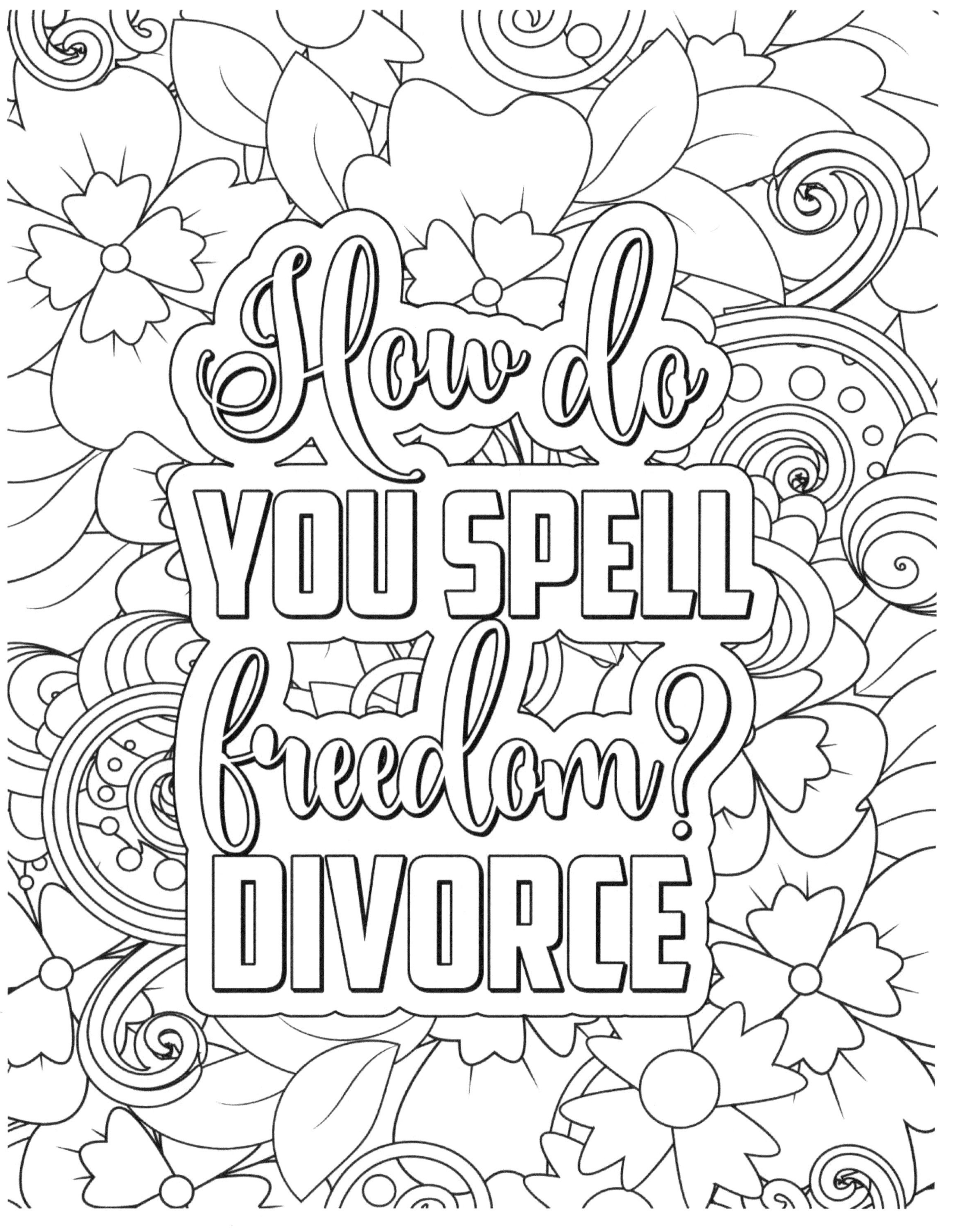

How do
YOU SPELL
freedom?
DIVORCE

IF, YOU'RE
happy & know
THANK YOU
Ex (clap, clap)

Been there.
Done That.
Divorced It.

Don't
Mess
With My
Energy.

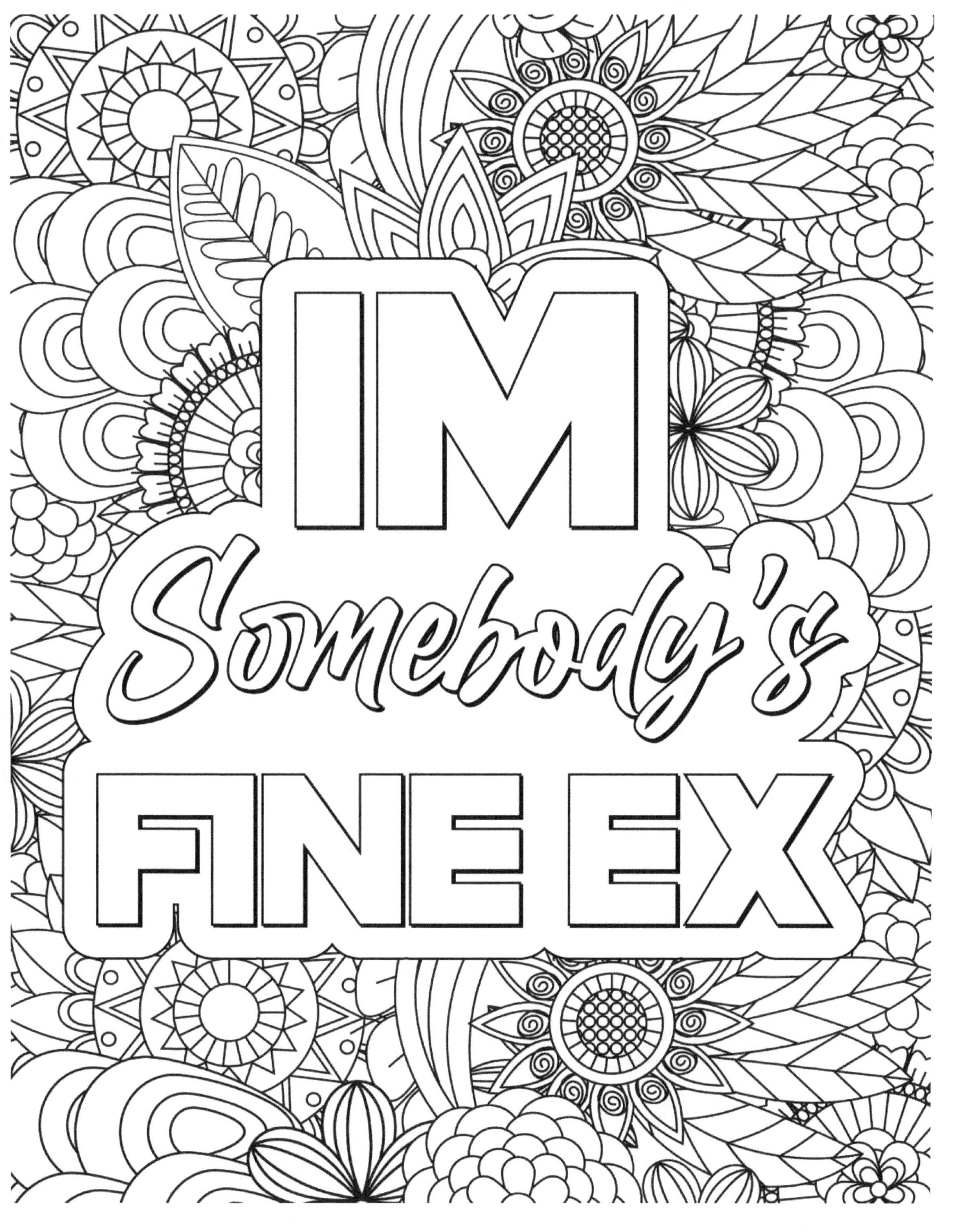

IM
Somebody's
FINE EX

Your
Vagina
Deserved
Better.

And She
LIVED
Happily
EVER
AFTER

FINALLY DIVORCED.

I Did.
I Do.
I'm Done.

Let
it Go.

NACHO
wife
ANYMORE

I Never
Liked Him.

DIVORCE:
better than
STARING
in a true crime
PODCAST.

NOBODY
LIKED HIM
ANYWAY.

HELLO TO YOUR NEW LIFE.

MARRIAGE:
ONE STAR.
WOULD NOT
RECOMMEND.

You Faked
EVERY
Orgasm
ANYWAY

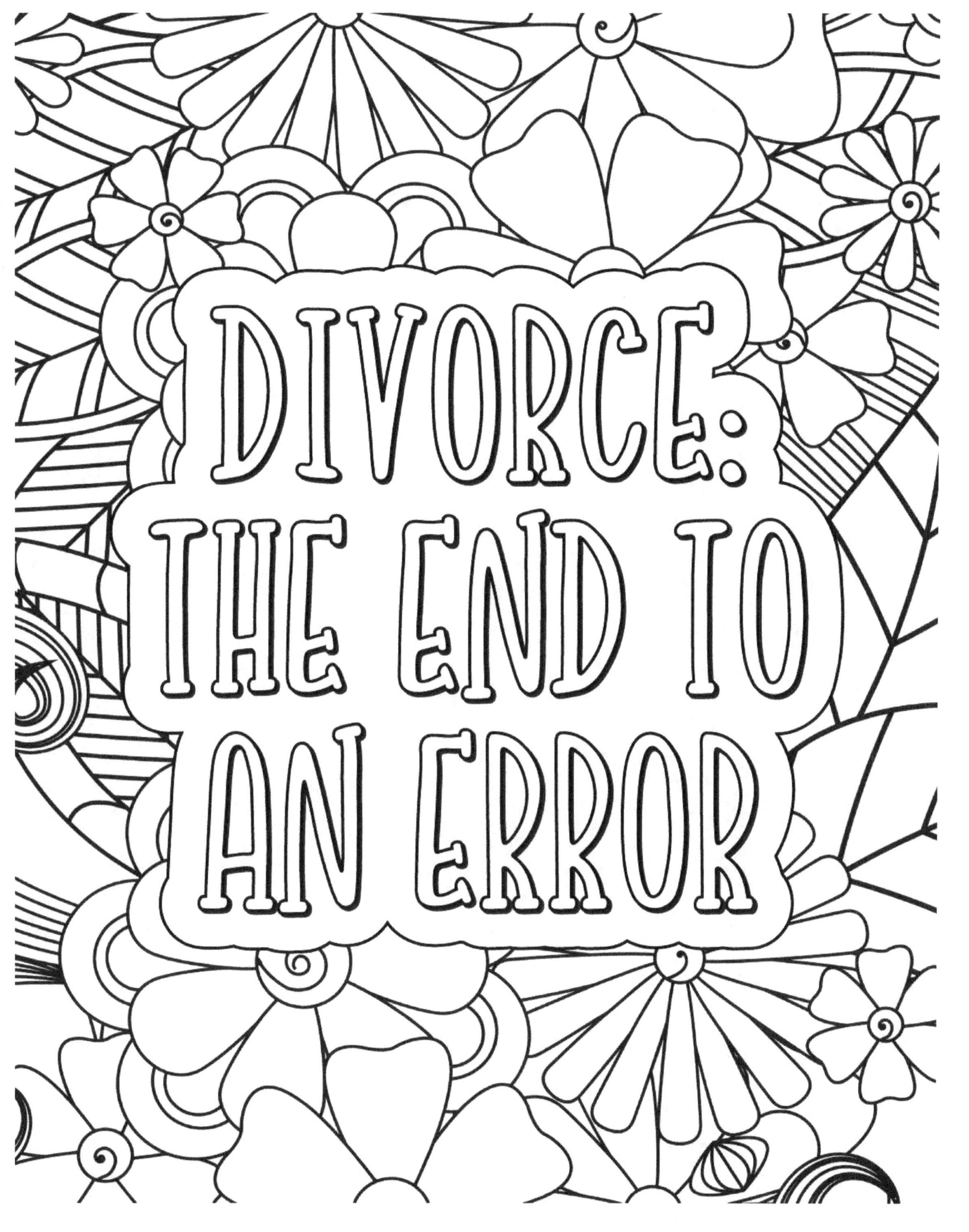
DIVORCE:
THE END TO
AN ERROR

He Didn't
DIE BUT
He's Dead
TO ME

SOMEONE
Now Thinks
YOUR TRASH IS
a Treasure

IT IS BETTER
To Have Love and
LOST THAN
To Be Stuck With
THEM FOREVER

CHEERS
TO LIVING
YOUR
BEST LIFE!

AND SHE
Lived Happily
EVER
After - Divorced

MAYBE NOW
You Will Truly
KNOW WHAT
Seven Inches
LOOKS LIKE

LIFE IS
tough,
BUT YOU
are too

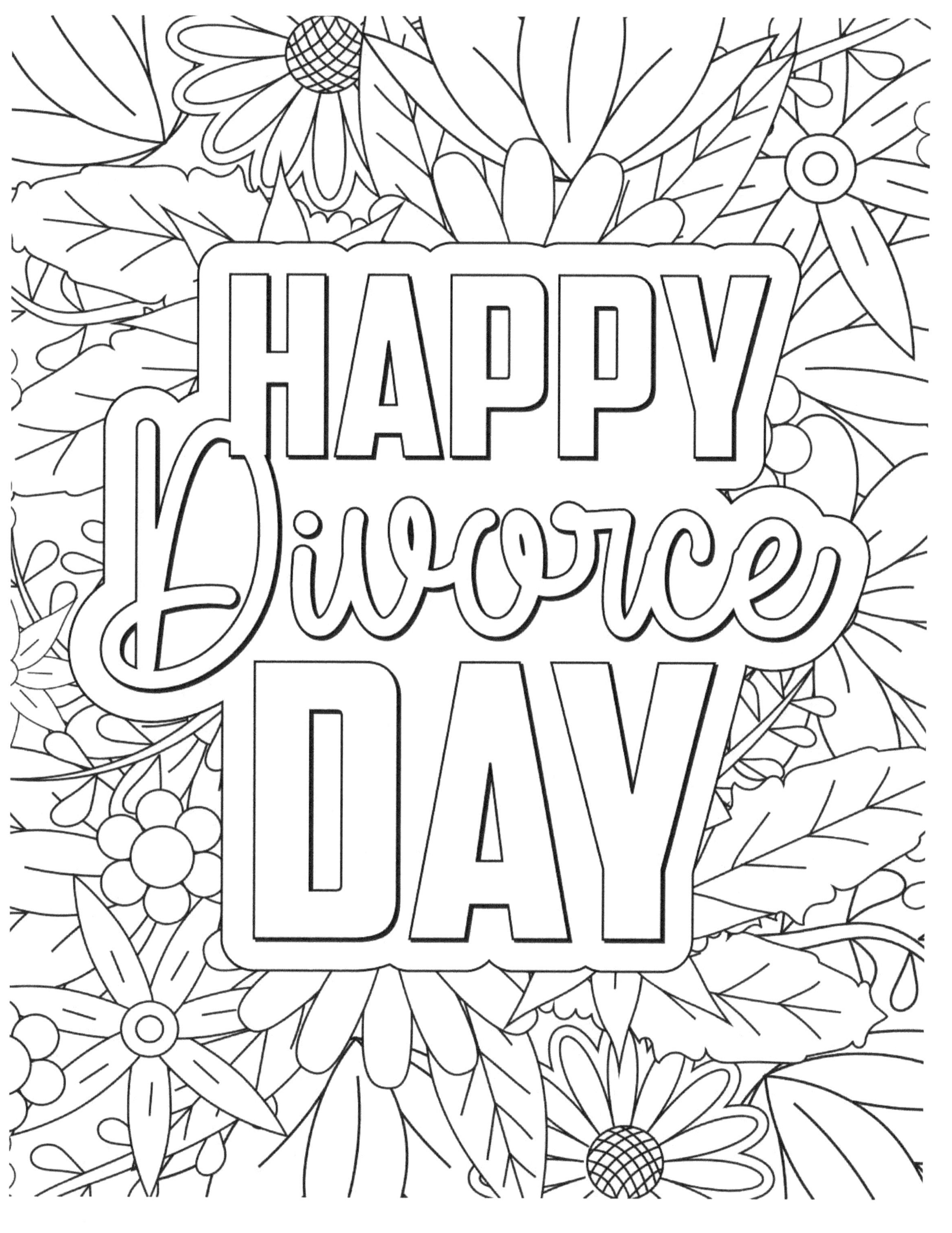

HAPPY
Divorce
DAY

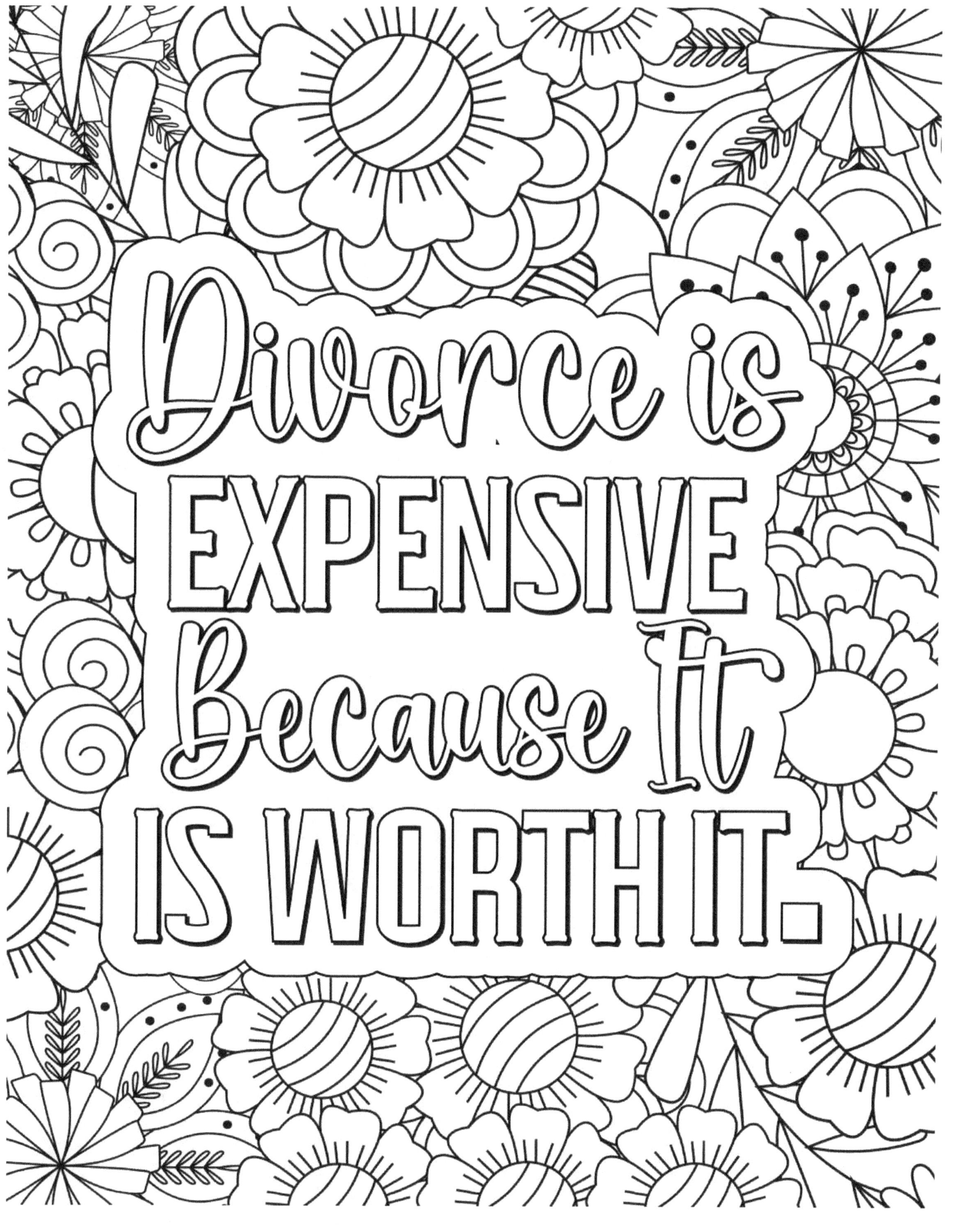

Divorce is
EXPENSIVE
Because It
IS WORTH IT.

Kiss The
MRS.
Goodbye

I USED TO
BE MARRIED,
BUT I'M
BETTER NOW.

Screw
HIM - JUST
Kidding - You
DON'T HAVE
To Anymore

BYE BYE
TEENIE
WEENIE

DON'T CRY
because
IT'S OVER.
laugh because
THEY ARE
someone else's
PROBLEM

THANKFUL
IT'S OVER

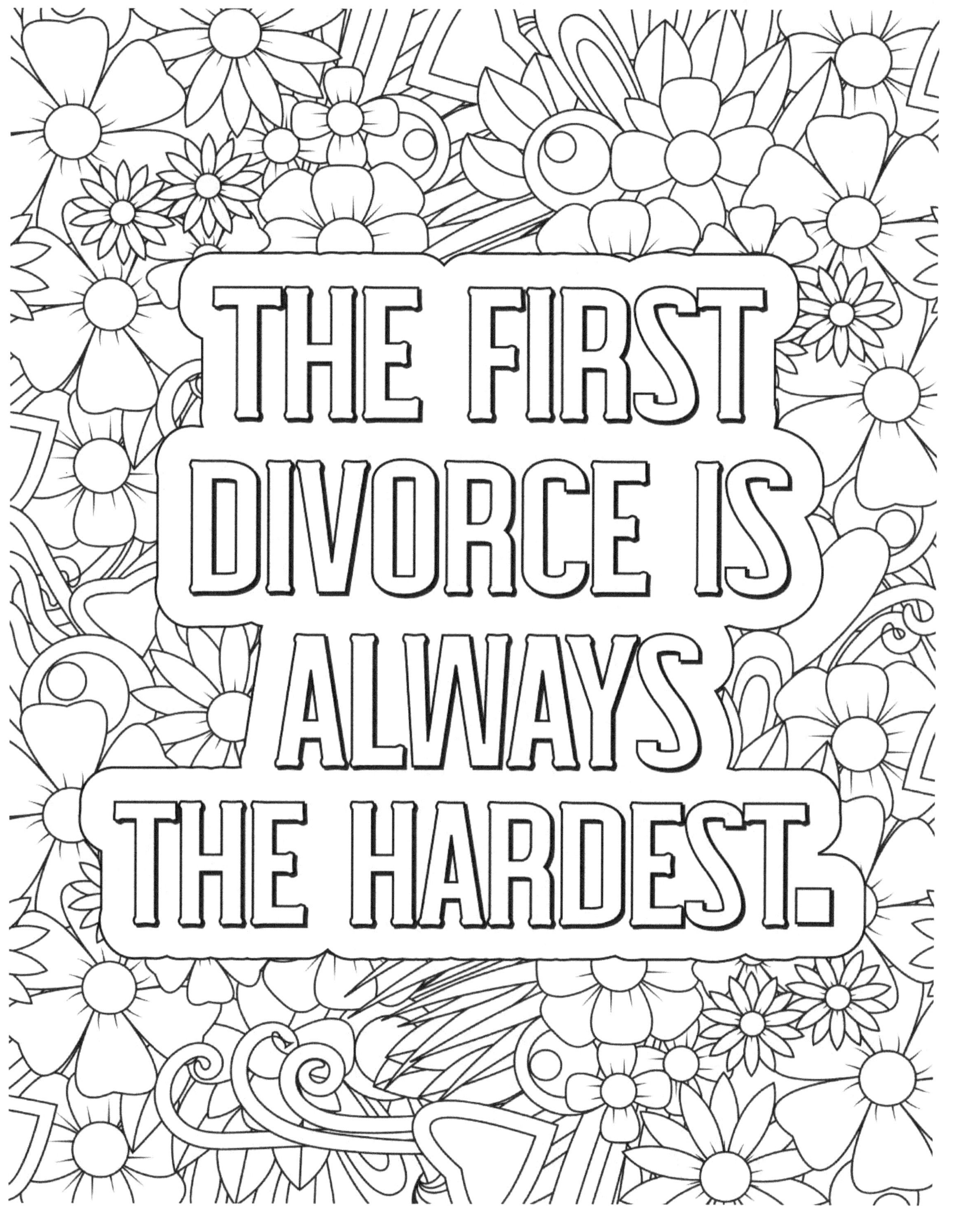

THE FIRST
DIVORCE IS
ALWAYS
THE HARDEST.

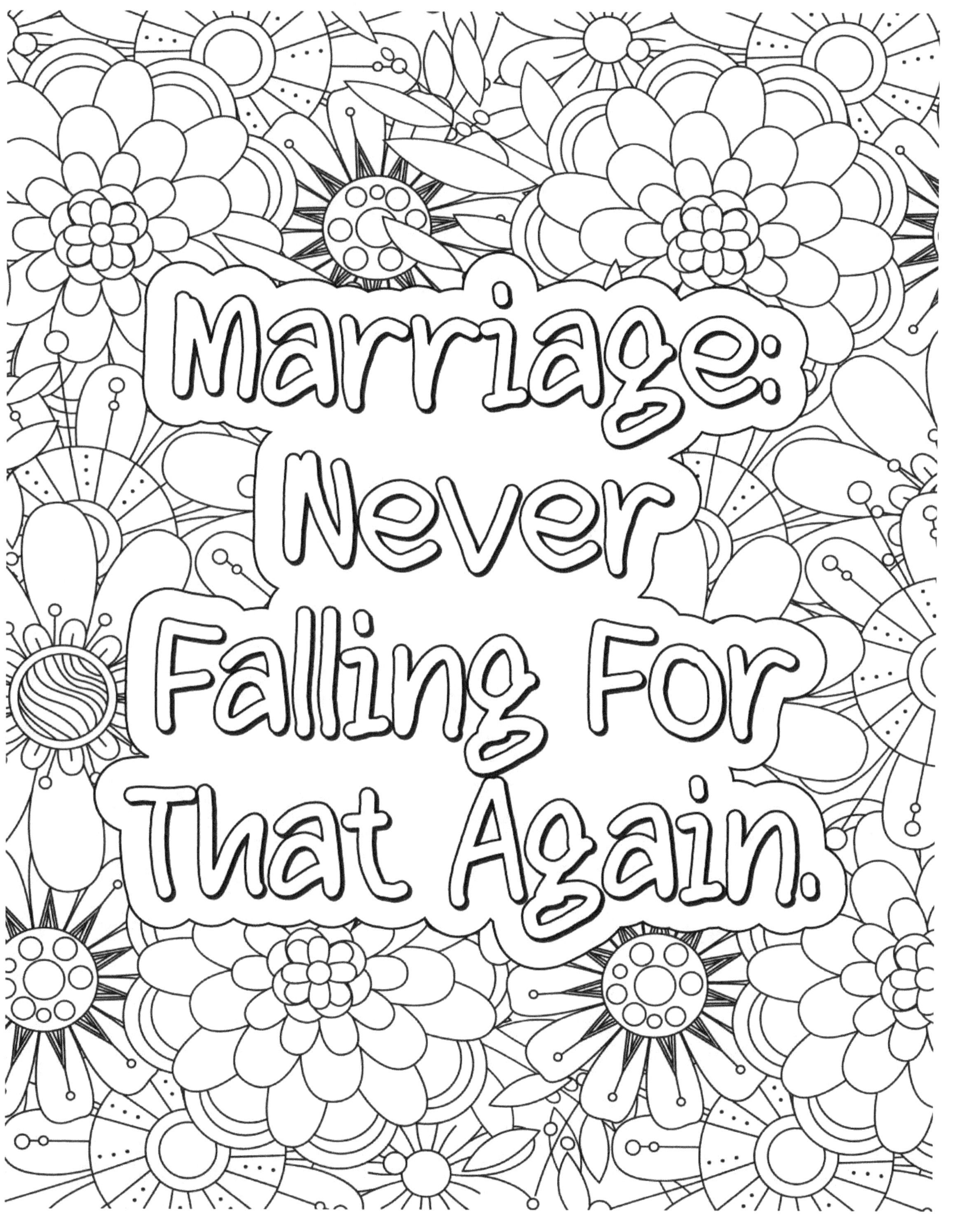

Marriage: Never Falling For That Again.